For our next generation (twins and all)—
Phillip and Sophia, Kerilynne and Hanna, Tristan and Reese—for whom we are all extremely thankful
—D.S.

In memory of my grandmother Marie Oliver Berry.
A lover of history and adventure.
—H.B.

Thanksgiving on Plymouth Plantation Text copyright © 2004 by Diane Stanley Illustrations copyright © 2004 by Holly Berry Manufactured in China. All rights reserved. For information address HarperCollins Children's Books, a division of HarperCollins Publishers, 195 Broadway, New York, NY 10007.
www.harperchildrens.com Library of Congress Cataloging-in-Publication Data Stanley, Diane. Thanksgiving on Plymouth Plantation / by Diane Stanley ; illustrated by Holly Berry. p.   cm. — (The time-traveling twins) Summary: Twins Liz and Lenny, along with their time-traveling grandmother, visit Plymouth Plantation to see how the Pilgrims lived and to celebrate a big feast with the Pilgrims and Native Americans. ISBN 0-06-027069-1 — ISBN 0-06-027076-4 (lib. bdg.) 1. Pilgrims (New Plymouth Colony)—Juvenile fiction. 2. Plymouth (Mass.)—History—Fiction. [1. Pilgrims (New Plymouth Colony)—Fiction. 2. Plymouth (Mass.)—History—Fiction. 3. Thanksgiving Day—Fiction. 4. Holidays—Fiction. 5. Time travel—Fiction.] I. Berry, Holly, ill. II. Title. PZ7.S7869 Th 2004 [Fic]—dc21 2002020548 Typography by Alicia Mikles
16 17 18 SCP 10 9

◆ THE TIME~TRAVELING TWINS ◆
Thanksgiving on Plymouth Plantation

By DIANE STANLEY   *Illustrated by* HOLLY BERRY

JOANNA COTLER BOOKS
An Imprint of HarperCollinsPublishers

Every year we go to visit our grandmother for Thanksgiving.
You're probably saying, "So what? Lots of people do that!"
And you're right. Lots of people do.
But you see, visiting our grandmother is not like visiting
your grandmother. *Our* grandmother takes us traveling,
and we don't mean to the Grand Canyon or
the Empire State Building.
She takes us traveling through time—
out west on the Oregon Trail or up to Boston for a tea party!
I'll bet your grandmother doesn't do that!

Mom and Dad decided to drive out into the country to get some apple cider at Whipple's Orchard. They asked if we wanted to come along. We said we'd rather stay home with Grandma. Then, as soon as they pulled out of the driveway, we begged Grandma to take us somewhere.

Why, Liz, what a great choice! That's Remember Allerton. She was your grandpa's great-great-great-great—well, I forget exactly how many greats it was—aunt. She was one of the Pilgrims who came over on the Mayflower.

My turn! My turn! I want to visit her!

Remember? What a weird name!

That's nothing! I know a dog named Sparkplug.

When you travel back in time, you have to put on the kind of clothes that people wore back then.
If you don't, they'll think you're really strange.

As soon as we were dressed, Grandma put on her magic hat
and we all held hands and closed our eyes.
She told us to take a deep breath—then, all of a sudden,
everything felt different. There was a cool breeze and
the air smelled woodsy.

Plymouth Plantation,
here we come!

Where we get
to meet our
forefathers!

And our
foremothers.

And our
foredogs.

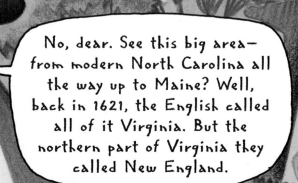

The first people we met were two boys.
They ran into the woods, laughing, like
they had just played a big joke on somebody—
and were they ever surprised to see us!
After all, the nearest English settlement
was at Jamestown, Virginia, hundreds
of miles to the south.
Grandma made up a story about
how we had sailed up from Jamestown
and our ship had sprung a leak.

Of course. Governor
Bradford will welcome
you—we could use your
help with the harvest.

So can we stay
here in Plymouth
for a while?

Why do they call themselves Pilgrims, anyway?
They don't, Lenny. They call themselves planters—because they came here to build, or "plant," a new colony. Many years later people started calling them Pilgrims since they traveled all this way because of their religion—that's what the word "pilgrim" means, you know.
I'm confused!

Governor Bradford was surprised to see us, too.
But he invited us to stay there and share what little they had.
He said that since it was harvesttime, they could really use our help.
When Grandma said we were distantly related to the Allerton family,
he said we should stay with them.

Come, I'll take you to see Isaac Allerton—he will be glad of a woman's help at home, I know. His wife, Mary, died this winter, and he has three children to look after.

Of course, I'd be happy to help.

If this is harvesttime, does that mean we get to go to the first Thanksgiving?

Well, sort of. You'll see.

A lot of people lived with Mr. Allerton. There was Isaac
Allerton and his three children—Bartholomew, Remember,
and little Mary. But some of them weren't relatives at all. They were
people whose families had died or who had come to America alone.
The house was just one big room with a fireplace at one end.
That's where they did their cooking. It was dark inside because
the windows were small. And they didn't even have glass in them—
just paper soaked in linseed oil. The floor was made of packed-down dirt.
There weren't enough chairs for everybody, so we sat down on whatever
was handy.

Yikes, it's cold
in here. And—
ouch!—something
just bit me!

Sorry, dear.
Could be fleas.
Could be lice.

You've got to
be kidding!

Gosh, Bartholomew—why did you come here anyway?
So we could practice our religion freely. Back in England it was against the law to have our own separate church, you know. They could put us in jail for it. So we escaped to Holland.
But it was too hard to make a living there. Now we're starting over again, and it's a lot of work—but we will own land and build a good life here.

Most of us slept on mattresses on the floor.

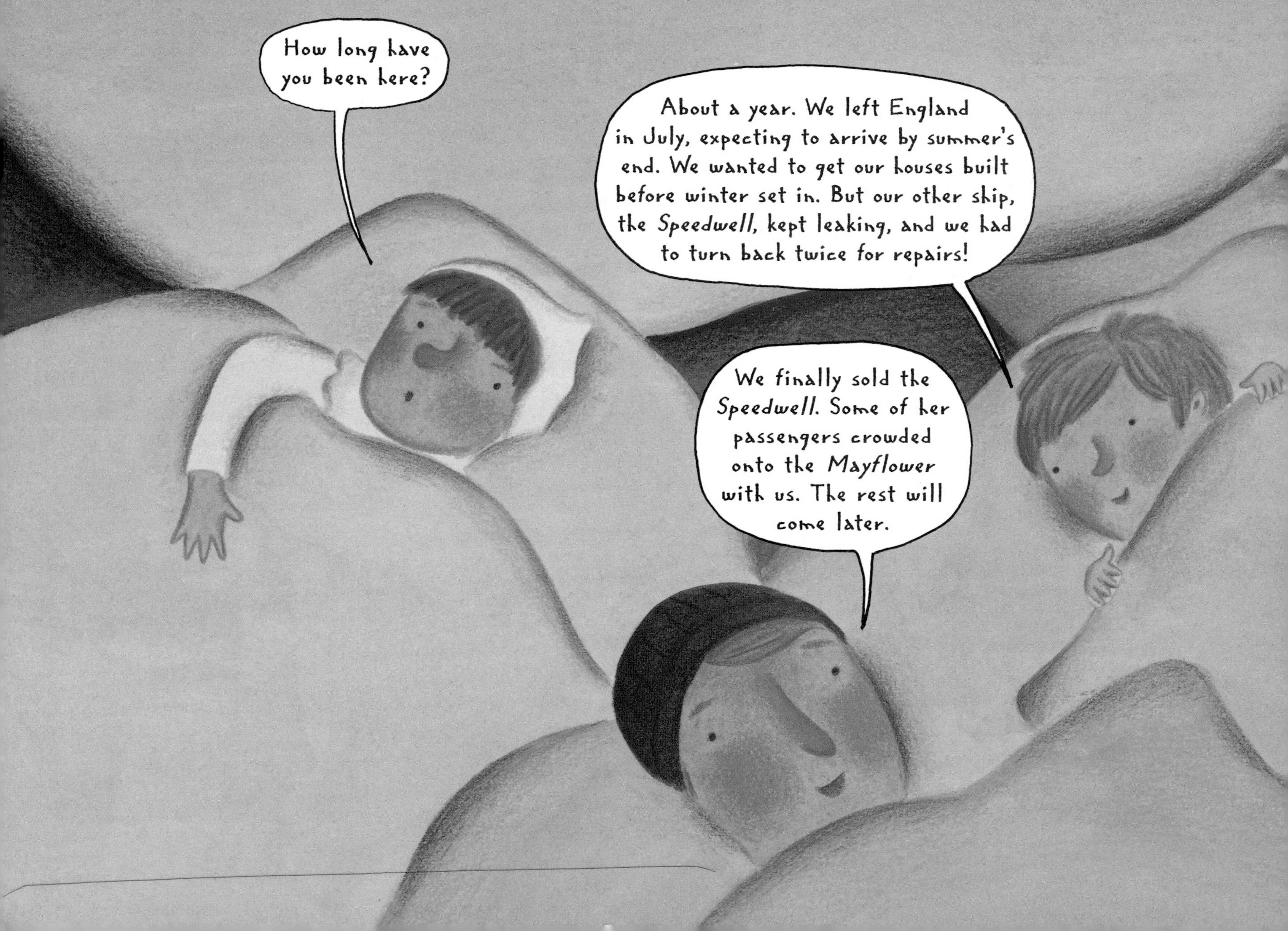

Nobody had pajamas. They just wore their long shirts and curled up under "bed rugs."

We got up early the next morning,
and everybody had a job to do.
We went down to the spring to fetch water.
Others brought in wood for the fire
or fed the chickens
or milked the goat
or picked sallet herbs (that's vegetables) from the garden.
Grandma helped make breakfast—but don't imagine
pancakes and bacon! It was mostly leftovers
(which they called relics)—goose broth,
and goat's milk cheese, and porridge
made from Indian corn.

We don't have school. But we hope to bring a schoolmaster over from England soon. For now, Papa is teaching us to read whenever he has the time. Even Mary is learning—aren't you, Mary?

Yes.

What time does school start?

It seemed like everything we did had to do with food.
As soon as breakfast was over, the women got busy
cooking the main meal of the day, which was served at noon.
The rest of us went out to collect food.
In the fields we gathered corn, then brought it back
to the house, where we hung it up until it was needed
to grind into cornmeal.

This is weird-looking corn—it's all different colors!

Yow! That's a *lot* of salt! Why are you doing that?

Salt dries out the fish and preserves it—so it will last through the winter.

We picked barley and, of course, lots of pompions. (Can you guess what those were? Pumpkins!) Other people went out hunting or fishing or gathering clams and mussels and eels.

It's Indian corn, child. It grows much better here than our English grains. And it will feed us through the winter.

We met a man called Squanto, a Wampanoag of the Patuxet village.
He spoke very good English because he used to live in London.
When he was a boy, some English sailors kidnapped him
and made him a slave.
But Squanto escaped and finally got back home.
When he arrived, he found his village deserted.
Many of his people had died from a terrible disease—
maybe smallpox—caught from European fishermen.

I lived in another village for a time. But since the English came, I have lived near them. They were in great need of my help, since they know little of our land and less of our language.

Oh, what a sad story! What happened then?

His name is actually Tisquantum, but I guess the English couldn't quite pronounce it.

And indeed, he has been a true friend to us! He taught us how to grow corn by digging holes, dropping a few fish inside, then planting the corn on top. That gives the corn something to feed upon as it grows.
But we had to keep an armed watch on the fields at night—so the wolves wouldn't dig up the fish and spoil our crop!

On Sunday we didn't work at all. That was the Lord's Day. As soon as we heard the drum beating, we knew it was time for church. We met at the house of Captain Myles Standish, the military leader of the colony. Then we lined up by threes and marched to church. Everybody in town was expected to go (even if they weren't church members), and the service lasted all morning. Then after lunch (which they called dinner) we went back for *three more* hours!

Which one's the minister?

You know who he is, dear—he's Love and Wrestling Brewster's father.
We don't have one yet. Until we do, Master Brewster acts as our religious leader. He's our ruling elder, you see.
Yeah, I was wondering about them. I mean, Love is a pretty weird name, especially for a boy, but at least it's kind of nice. But why would anyone name their kid Wrestling?
I believe it's short for Wrestling-with-the-Devil.
I take it back. That definitely beats Sparkplug.

The Puritans didn't have anything in their worship service that wasn't mentioned in the Bible. So there weren't any prayer books or hymns. There wasn't an altar with candles. There wasn't any *heat*, either, so some people brought little foot warmers filled with burning coals.
We kids sat with the women
and were expected to keep quiet.
The only time we got to open our mouths
was to sing psalms and say "Amen."

This doesn't look like a church—it looks more like a storeroom.

It *is* a storeroom. But the building isn't important. It is the *people* who are the church.

Children—hush!

Mmmmm, cozy!

At last the harvest was all gathered in, and it was time to celebrate.
So the men went off hunting and fishing
and came back with enough food to last us all for a week.
The women worked just as hard chopping and mixing,
boiling and frying. They made stews (which they called pottages),
roasted meat on spits over the fire,
and stuffed "puddings" into the bellies of the turkeys.

Puddings?

That's stuffing
to you.

The guest of honor was Massasoit,
a sachem (or chief) of the Wampanoag people.
He arrived with about ninety men,
and they stayed and ate with us for three days.
Some of the men who came with Massasoit
went hunting and brought back five deer
as gifts for the most important colonists.
Even with such a big crowd,
there was plenty of food.

Look, there he is—the king of the Indians!

We have a treaty with Massasoit, you know—signed last spring. We agreed to help them if they are attacked, and they promised to do the same for us.

"Massasoit" isn't actually his name—it's his title. It means "great leader." His real name is Ousamequin, which means "yellow feather" in Wampanoag.

Of course nobody had a table big enough to seat one hundred and forty people, so we ate all over the place. The important men, like Governor Bradford and Captain Standish and Massasoit, sat at the head table and had the best food. The rest of us ate inside or outside, at tables or on the ground. It was kind of like a big potluck supper. We helped set the tables and serve the food and clear the dishes away— that's what children and unmarried young people were expected to do.

I'm hungry. When do we get to eat?

I don't understand—why do John and William and Edward and George have to do so much work, while the other men just sit there?

Why—because they're servants, Liz.

Nobody ate with forks in those days.
They used knives to slice off bits of meat,
and they had spoons.
But mostly they just ate with their hands.
It's a good thing they had those huge napkins!
The plates were called trenchers,
and most of them were made of wood.

What's the matter—
don't you like your
stewed eel?

Umm . . . I
think I'd rather
have turkey.

Just think! Here we are at the first Thanksgiving!
This isn't a Thanksgiving, Liz—it's a harvest festival, like the ones we had back in England. A Day of Thanksgiving is a religious holiday, when we spend the day in church.
Bartholomew is right. The people of Plymouth won't have a true Day of Thanksgiving until July 1623—when a good rain arrives and ends a long drought that had threatened their crops.

After dinner we played games,
like stool-ball and pitching the bar.
We had races and wrestling matches.

While we were busy playing games,
the men "exercised their arms."
That doesn't mean they did push-ups;
it means they shot at targets with their muskets.

Finally Massasoit and his men thanked us for a nice party
and went home to their village.
We took down the tables and washed the tablecloths,
and everybody got back to life as usual.

They had been through a hard first year and had another hard winter ahead.

We hated to say good-bye to our new friends, especially Remember and Bartholomew. But we had to go home and help Grandma cook Thanksgiving dinner.

So Grandma put on her magic hat,
and faster than you can say "Happy Thanksgiving,"
we were back at Grandma's house.
A few minutes after that, Mom and Dad came home
with a bag of apples and two gallons of cider.

AUTHOR'S NOTE

So if the meal the English shared with the Wampanoag in the fall of 1621 wasn't the first Thanksgiving held on these shores (or wasn't even a Thanksgiving at all), then what *was*? It surely took place long before Europeans came to America, when Native people held ceremonies to give thanks for the sun and stars, the wind and rain, the animals and the gift of life.

Claims for the first Thanksgiving in America celebrated by *Europeans* include one held by Ponce de León in Florida back in 1513, and another by Francisco Vásquez de Coronado in the Texas Panhandle in 1541. Others make claims for first Thanksgivings in Newfoundland, El Paso, Maine, and Jamestown. The first *national* day of Thanksgiving, declared by the Continental Congress, was on Thursday, December 18, 1777.

In October of 1863, though "in the midst of a civil war of unequaled magnitude and severity," President Abraham Lincoln still felt there was much the nation should be grateful for. He declared a national day of Thanksgiving to be held on the last Thursday in November. We have been celebrating it ever since.

The 1621 harvest celebration wasn't referred to as the "First Thanksgiving" until 1841, and it wasn't until after 1900 that the story of the Pilgrims peacefully sharing a turkey dinner with the Wampanoag became associated in the American mind with our annual Thanksgiving Day.

To learn more about Plymouth Plantation and the First Thanksgiving, you can visit Plimoth Plantation, Inc., a private nonprofit living history museum in Plymouth, Massachusetts—or visit them on the web at www.plimoth.org.

—D.S.